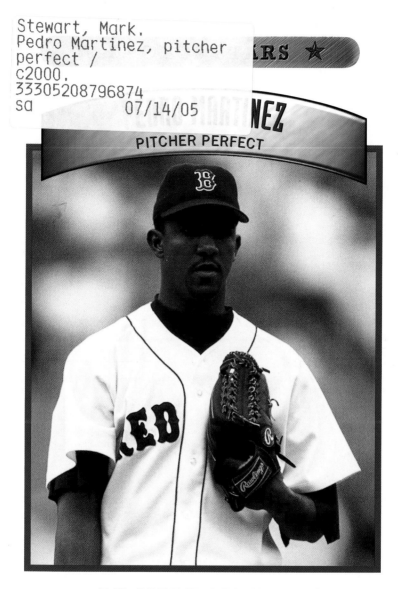

STARS ★

PEDRO MARTINEZ

PITCHER PERFECT

BY MARK STEWART

New York · · · · · · · · · · · · · · Sydney
Mexico City · · · · · · Hong Kong
Danbury, Connecticut

Photo Credits
Photographs ©: AllSport USA: 31; AP/Wide World Photos: 33, 45 left (Neal Hamberg), 41 (Phil Long), 30 (Julia Malakie), 29 (Steve Nesius), 42 (John Riley), 46 (Jim Rogash), 38, 43 (Steven Senne), 32 (Bill Sikes); Corbis-Bettmann: 37, 45 right (Reuters Newmedia Inc.); Icon Sports Media: 3 (David Seelig); John Klein: cover, 25, 26; Mel Bailey: 15, 20, 44 left; SportsChrome East/West: 47 (Scott Cunningham), 12 (Louis A. Raynor), 6, 44 right.

Library of Congress Cataloging-in-Publication Data

Stewart, Mark.
    Pedro Martinez, pitcher perfect / by Mark Stewart.
      p. cm. — (Sports stars)
      Summary: A biography of the Boston Red Sox pitcher who won the Cy Young Award in 1997 and 1999.
      ISBN 0-516-22048-9 (lib. bdg.)   0-516-27073-7 (pbk.)
      1. Martinez, Pedro, 1971---Juvenile literature. 2. Baseball players— Dominican Republic—Biography—Juvenile literature. [1. Martinez, Pedro, 1971- 2. Baseball players. 3. Dominicans (Dominican Republic)— Biography.] I. Series.

GV865.M355 S74 2000
796.357'092—dc21
[B]

                                            00-020808

CONTENTS ✶

★ 1 ★

THE INTIMIDATOR

The fans are on their feet, the bleachers are shaking, Dominican flags are waving furiously, and the noise is earsplitting. This can mean only one thing: Pedro Martinez is on the mound and the game is on the line.

Despite the commotion, Pedro looks completely calm. His friends and family watching on television know that face—it is the same one he wears when he stretches out in the branches of the big mango tree on his farm back home.

This is not good news for the batter. He knows Pedro is in control. He has already watched an outside fastball dart back over home plate for strike one. And he flinched in terror at a curveball that started toward his ribs but ended up in the catcher's glove for strike two.

Believing Pedro will challenge him with a fastball, the batter stands ready to uncoil as soon as the pitch leaves Pedro's hand. Pedro rocks and delivers. His right arm whips forward and the batter begins his swing. But the ball is not where it should be—it is floating softly toward the plate. The batter tries in vain to slow down his swing, but the bat crosses home plate an instant before the ball arrives. Strike three!

The stadium roars to life. The air is filled with 50,000 screaming voices. Pedro walks off the mound with another victory. He has more than 100 wins already, and he is just beginning the prime years of his career. Pedro Martinez is a manager's dream . . . and a hitter's nightmare.

★ 2 ★

BROTHERS IN ARMS

Pedro Martinez grew up just outside Santo Domingo, the capital city of the Dominican Republic, in a town called Manoguayabo. He was one of four boys who shared a tiny three-room house with two sisters, their mother, and their father. "Our parents cared for us and did a great job instilling values in us," says Pedro. "We grew up poor, very poor. But I am very proud of where I come from."

No matter how little money the Martinez family had, Pedro's parents—Paulino and Leopoldina—always made sure their children were dressed neatly for school. Pedro enjoyed

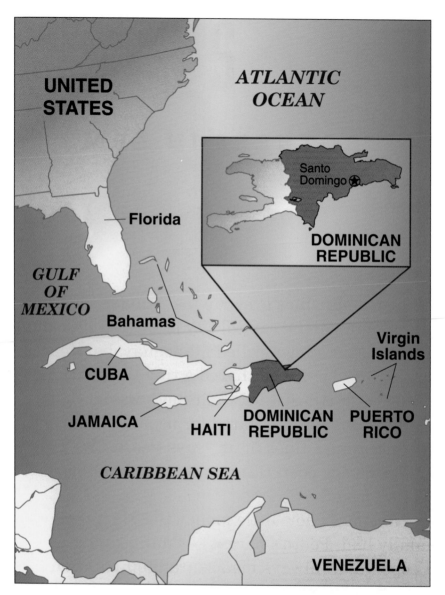

Pedro grew up just outside the Dominican Republic's capital city, Santo Domingo, in a town called Manoguayabo.

his classes, and did especially well in English. "The lowest grade I ever had was a 98," he says proudly. "I was straight aces!"

Pedro's father had been quite a pitcher in his youth. He was a teammate of the famous Alou brothers—Felipe, Mateo, and Jesus—and was known throughout the Dominican Republic for his curveball and sinker. Some say he could have been a major leaguer, but when the San Francisco Giants offered him a tryout he had no cleats, so he could not go.

Pedro's brothers—Ramon, Nelson, and Jesus—were also pitchers. So, naturally, Pedro wanted to be a pitcher too. Unlike his brothers, Pedro was not big and tall. He had a smaller build and a more delicate body. He considered himself the "runt of the family," and because of his size, he did not think he had a chance to become a star.

Pedro's brother, Ramon, was signed by the Dodgers in 1984. Ramon reached the majors the same year the team signed Pedro.

★ ★ ★

Just before Pedro's 13th birthday, the Martinez family received spectacular news— Ramon was selected to represent the Dominican Republic at the 1984 Olympics in Los Angeles. Right after the games, the Los Angeles Dodgers signed him to a contract. Pedro tagged along when Ramon reported to the team's training camp in Santo Domingo. "One day the pitching coach there in the camp decided to take the [radar] gun and put it on me," Pedro recalls. "I was at 77 to 80 [miles per hour]. He said I could be a professional pitcher if I worked at it."

Encouraged, Pedro began taking the game seriously and practiced hard to become a better pitcher. In the spring of 1988, just before he turned 17, the Dodgers signed him to a minor-league contract.

★ 3 ★

LITTLE GUY, BIG SKY

For two seasons, Pedro pitched in the Dominican Summer League. He won 12 games and lost just 3. During this time he attended college, where he learned to speak English really well. In 1990, the Dodgers decided Pedro was ready to play in the United States, and shipped him to their Pioneer League team in Great Falls, Montana.

Pedro had never seen anything like Montana. As the team traveled from town to town, he took in the breathtaking landscapes and marveled at how the mountains towered over everything.

Pedro's great year for Great Falls in 1990 earned him a promotion to Bakersfield in 1991.

They don't call this "Big Sky" country for
nothing, he thought. Pedro did well at Great
Falls, going 8–3 for a team that had the second-
best winning percentage in all of pro baseball.
Pedro's teammates that year included future
star Raul Mondesi.

Though Pedro was small for a "power"
pitcher, he could throw his fastball over
90 miles per hour. His secret was his smooth,
compact motion. The only thing that looked
like it might hold Pedro back was his weight.
He was so skinny that the team threatened
to fine him $500 if they caught him running
laps. A tireless worker, Pedro had to convince
the stadium security guard to let him in late
at night to work out.

Despite Pedro's good work in 1990, all his
friends and family talked about after the season
was how well his brother, Ramon, was doing. In
his first full season with the Dodgers, Ramon
chalked up 20 victories and pitched more

complete games than anyone in baseball. Pedro received praise too, but he knew no one thought he would ever be as good as Ramon.

Deep down, though, Pedro believed he was every bit as good as Ramon, and in 1991 he set out to prove it. All told, Pedro pitched in 28 games during the 1991 season. His record was 18–8 and he struck out 192 batters in 177 1/3 innings. For his spectacular rise through the Dodgers farm system, Pedro was named *The Sporting News* Minor League Player of the Year.

★ 4 ★

WELCOME TO
THE MAJORS

After spending a full season with the Albuquerque Dukes in 1992, Pedro was promoted to the Dodgers in late September. He managed to get into two games—one as a starter and one as a reliever. What a thrill it was to be a big-leaguer at the age of 21.

Few fans realized it at the time, but Pedro nearly ended his career before it started— swinging a bat in practice! Pedro was just warming up near the batting cage that fall, when he heard something pop in his left shoulder. It was a serious injury, and it required reconstructive surgery. Luckily, it was not his pitching shoulder.

By spring training in 1993, Pedro was competing for a spot on the team. The Dodgers needed a right-handed pitcher who could come out of the bullpen and throw hard for several innings. Pedro did just that, but Los Angeles had one too many pitchers in camp, and, unfortunately, Pedro was the odd man out. Just before the team left to start the season, he was told that he would be going back to Albuquerque. Pedro was so disappointed that he thought about quitting. "I called and told my daddy that I was coming home," he remembers. "I couldn't take this."

Ramon reminded his brother that, five years earlier, he had pitched a shutout during his rookie year and was sent to the minors the very next day. Baseball is a business, he explained, and sometimes clubs make moves for reasons players do not understand. Pedro decided to stick it out, and the Dodgers recalled him after just one minor-league game.

Pedro's smooth, compact delivery enabled him to throw hard with little rest.

★ ★ ★

Pedro made good use of this second chance and had a great rookie year. He led Los Angeles pitchers with 65 games played. Pedro's most impressive statistic was the measly .165 batting average he allowed when runners were in scoring position. He also proved that, despite his size, he could throw a lot of innings. Even Pedro was a little amazed at how he held up during his first year. "Once I pitched three times in four days," he remembers. "Then we went to New York and I thought: Am I going to have to pitch today, too? I did—and I threw harder than I did all year!"

The team's fans could hardly wait for 1994, when both Martinez brothers would be in the starting rotation. Little did they know that the wheels were turning in the Dodgers' front office, and that Pedro was on the trading block. The Montreal Expos wanted the young right-hander, and in return they were offering something Los Angeles really needed: Delino Deshields, a second baseman who could hit and steal bases.

The rarest trade in baseball is one that
involves two young stars, but the Dodgers and
Expos decided to do it. When Pedro heard the
news, he was shocked and angry. "They said I
was the future of the Dodgers," he recalls. "I was
the one guy coming out of the minors who could
be a starter. I could have been anything they
wanted me to be."

After awhile though, Pedro began to see the
move to Montreal as a positive one. He would
be playing for the most respected Dominican
manager in the game—Felipe Alou, his dad's
old teammate. Pedro's warm smile and gentle
manner made the Montreal fans fall in love with
him before he even threw a pitch. And during a
publicity tour that winter, Pedro began falling in
love with Canada.

★ 5 ★

OH, CANADA

The Expos were a young team on the rise. Outfielders Marquis Grissom, Larry Walker, and Moises Alou were just entering their prime years, and prospects Rondell White, Cliff Floyd, and Wil Cordero seemed ready to contribute. The Montreal pitching staff was talented too. Pedro joined a rotation that included Ken Hill, Jeff Fassero, Kirk Rueter, and Butch Henry.

Playing in the National League's Eastern Division, the Expos had to contend with the powerhouse Atlanta Braves and the 1993 league champion Philadelphia Phillies. Alou told his players not to worry about these teams—if the Expos played hard and believed in themselves, good things would happen.

Alou was correct. By mid-season, the Expos had opened up a healthy lead over the Phillies and were several games ahead of the Braves. Pedro played a big part in the team's success. He blossomed into the top young starter in the league. In 1994, National League hitters were putting up record-setting numbers, but not against Pedro. On April 13, he carried a no-hitter against the Reds into the ninth inning before Brian Dorsett broke it up with a leadoff single.

Pedro might have won 20 games had the season not ended in mid-August due to a labor dispute between the owners and players. And the Expos might have won their division—they were ahead by six games when the season shut down.

In 1995, Pedro became the most feared and hated hurler in the league. Believing that a pitcher "owned" the inside portion of the strike zone, Pedro did not like it when batters stood too close to home plate. Several times in each game, he would send opponents sprawling to

Pedro could hardly wait to take the mound for Montreal, where he blossomed as a starter in 1994.

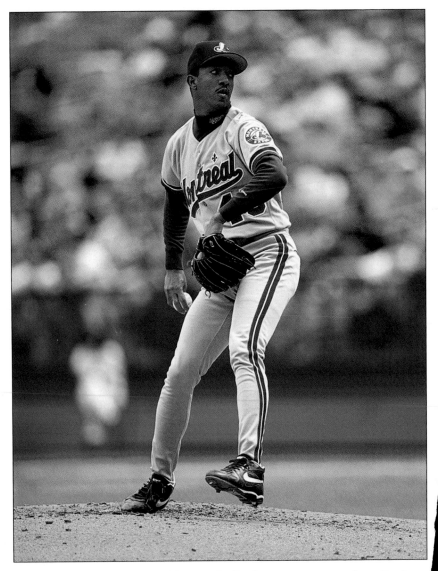

**Although throwing inside made Pedro many enemies, it also
made him a very successful pitcher.**

the ground. In the old days, all pitchers threw this way, but in recent years, pitchers have chosen to work batters "away." Pedro was an unwelcome blast from the past.

"I was never a headhunter," he insists. "Felipe Alou once said at a meeting that if anyone came out after me, he would be the first one on the field in my defense. He knew I wasn't trying to hurt anyone." The umpires warned Pedro to be more careful, and threatened to throw him out of games if he continued to terrorize hitters. Pedro felt horrible. Finally, he called Ramon.

Pedro's brother told him that there was nothing wrong with pitching inside. However, if he could not control his pitches, he should pitch low instead of high. He was less likely to get into trouble or start a fight if he threw at belt buckles instead of batting helmets. Pedro took Ramon's advice. Within two years, he was the National League's top pitcher and fans were calling him the "Intimidator."

★ 6 ★

HOLA, BOSTON

Unfortunately, as Pedro improved as a pitcher, the Expos got worse as a team. The problem was money. Montreal's attendance and television ratings were not as high as those of other teams, so the club made less money. Each year, the Expos were forced to let their best players join richer teams. This frustrated Pedro. He wanted to win a championship too. "At times I didn't want to be on this team anymore," he admits. "I wanted to be on a team that was going to be able to compete. There was always something missing in Montreal."

All an athlete can do in such situations is his best. In 1997, Pedro became just the fifth National Leaguer since 1900 to strike out more than 300 batters. He also won the Cy Young Award as the league's best pitcher. This honor meant a lot to Pedro. As a kid, he had idolized Dominican pitcher Juan Marichal. Despite winning 25 or more games three times during the 1960s, Marichal never received the Cy Young Award. All the boys in the

Dominican Republic grew up hearing the same thing: This was history's greatest injustice. So when Pedro met the Hall of Famer at a banquet that winter, he gave Juan his award!

Juan Marichal, the first Dominican player to enter the Hall of Fame

Pedro smiles for the cameras at his new address, Boston's historic Fenway Park.

But Pedro had little time to savor his super season. Having completed his fifth year in the majors, he was now eligible for a big pay raise. Pedro knew what that meant—the Expos would have to get rid of him. On November 18, he was traded to the Boston Red Sox. "To be honest, I was disappointed when they first told me I was going to Boston," Pedro admits, but that would change within a matter of days.

Pedro flew to Boston to attend a press conference announcing the deal, and got a warm reception the moment he stepped off the airplane.

Several hundred fans were waiting for him at Logan International Airport. They clapped and shouted and held up signs welcoming him to the team. "That really shocked me," Pedro says. "I didn't know anyone would recognize me. That night I said to someone, 'I think I love Boston already.'"

Pedro also loved the team he was joining. The 1998 Red Sox had some great players—Mo Vaughn had won the Most Valuable Player (MVP) award in 1995 and Nomar Garciaparra had led

Slugger Nomar Garciaparra, the hitting star of the Boston Red Sox

Jimy Williams knew Pedro well from his days as a coach for the Atlanta Braves.

the league in hits as a rookie in 1997. The manager, Jimy Williams, was a master at getting the most out of his players. Finally, Pedro was on a team that could contend for the pennant. Of course, the demanding Red Sox fans expected Pedro to deliver that pennant—especially after he signed a contract that made him the highest-paid player in baseball history!

Before reporting to spring training, Pedro spent some of his newfound wealth to pay for construction of a brand-new church in his hometown of Manoguayabo. "The people mobbed me and hugged me, the priest blessed me, everyone had tears in their eyes—it was unbelievable," Pedro says of the opening ceremony.

Pedro did everything his first season in Boston except pitch the Red Sox to the pennant. He finished second in the league in ERA and strikeouts, and won 19 games while losing just 7.

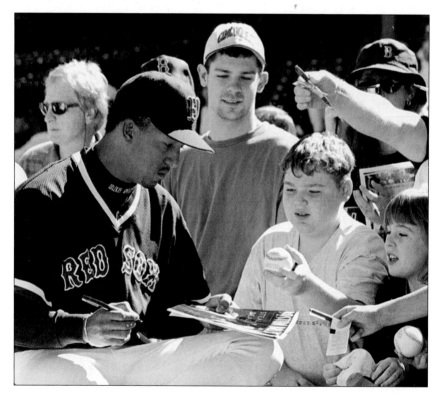

Pedro connected with Boston fans immediately. He quickly became their favorite pitcher.

But this was the year the New York Yankees won an astounding 114 games. The Red Sox, whose 92 victories were the second-highest total in the American League (A.L.), made the playoffs as the Wild Card. Pedro baffled the Cleveland Indians in the opening game of the series, but Cleveland bounced back to win the next three games, dashing the pennant hopes of the Boston fans.

That winter, Pedro went home to begin his "second season." The Martinez brothers are considered national treasures, and fans in the Dominican Republic yearn to see them play. Because their contracts prohibit them from pitching in the winter, the brothers formed their own softball team. They tour the Dominican Republic, often playing teams sponsored by other major leaguers, such as Pedro's next door neighbor, Juan Guzman. Ramon usually plays first base, Jesus patrols center field, and Pedro is the designated hitter.

⋆ 7 ⋆

SUPER SEASON

During the 1999 season, baseball fans across America celebrated the great players and fantastic feats of an unforgettable century of baseball. In ballparks everywhere, Hall of Famers were honored in elaborate ceremonies. However, few of these all-time legends ever put together the kind of season Pedro had in 1999. He won 15 times in the first half, beating some of the top teams in the majors. Some thought Pedro might become the first man in more than 30 years to win 30 games.

With the All-Star Game scheduled for Boston's Fenway Park, Pedro was the obvious choice to start for the American League. As he took the mound to the thunderous applause of the hometown fans, he felt a surge of adrenaline rush through his body. The A.L. beat the National League (N.L.), 4–1, and Pedro was named All-Star MVP.

A sore shoulder bothered Pedro in the second half of the season, but he was still playing well. He won his 20th game against Seattle on September 4, striking out 15 Mariners in the process, then won three more times to finish the year 23–4. His best game of the year came against their arch rivals, the Yankees. He threw a brilliant one-hitter, striking out 12 of the final 15 batters to finish with a total of 17.

Pedro dominated every major pitching category in 1999. His 23 wins were five more than the runner-up; his 313 strikeouts were 113 more than the second-place finisher; and his 2.07 ERA was more than a full run better than the A.L.'s number-two pitcher.

Pedro struck out Sammy Sosa, Mark McGwire, and three other National League superstars to win the All-Star MVP award.

**Ramon Martinez returned from a major injury to help the
Red Sox nail down a playoff spot in the final weeks of the
1999 season.**

The highlight of Pedro's year came on August 31, when he and Ramon were reunited. Ramon had suffered a devastating arm injury a year earlier with the Dodgers. In March 1999, Pedro urged the Red Sox to sign him—despite what the doctors said, he knew his brother would recover. Ramon was a big help to the Red Sox in September, winning twice and allowing just three runs a game.

Once again, the Red Sox found themselves facing the Cleveland Indians in the first round of the playoffs. In the opening game, Pedro was pitching a shutout when he felt something snap in his back. Afraid to risk further injury, he pulled himself out of the game. With Pedro on the bench, the Indians came back to win. The following evening, the Indians won again to take a 2–0 lead in the best-of-five series. It looked like another quick October exit for the Red Sox.

But then the Boston bats came alive, and the Red Sox managed to tie the series 2–2. Pedro was still feeling tightness in his back, but told manager Jimy Williams he would try to pitch in Game Five. He could not say how long he might last. Williams brought Pedro into the ball game after the Indians had scored eight runs in three innings. He asked his injured star to give him an inning or two while the team regrouped. Pedro nodded. Then he went to work.

One by one, he mowed down the Cleveland hitters. Pedro did not have his good fastball, or his good curve. But he could smell a victory, and that was all he needed. Instead of pitching an inning or two, he finished the game—going six innings without allowing so much as a single hit! When baseball fans look back at the great individual achievements of the twentieth century, Pedro's "night of no hits" will rank right up there with the greatest.

Pedro is mobbed by teammates after six magnificent innings of no-hit ball against the mighty Cleveland Indians.

Pedro flashes two fingers to show he is receiving his second Cy Young Award.

A few days later, Pedro shut down the Yankees in Game Three of the League Championship Series. But Boston could not win more than that one game. New York advanced to the World Series, denying Pedro his greatest dream. He says he would trade all of his personal honors—including the Cy Young Award he received for his terrific 1999 season—for a chance to pitch in baseball's Fall Classic.

One day, he will make it. Of that he is certain. And when that day comes, Pedro cannot think of a better city to take with him than Boston, which he considers America's best baseball town. "This is a special place," he says. "I want to take my team to the top. That's my focus . . . that's really all I'm thinking about."

Pedro has been hearing it from the fans since the day he arrived in Boston. He hopes to give them a World Series championship.

C ★ H ★ R ★ O ★ N

1971 • July 25: Pedro is born in Manoguayabo, Dominican Republic.

1984 • Pedro's older brother Ramon pitches in the Olympics and signs with the Los Angeles Dodgers.

1986 • Pedro is discovered by scouts at Campo Las Palmas baseball academy in Santo Domingo.

1988 • Pedro is signed by the Dodgers at the age of 16.

1991 • Pedro is named Minor League Player of the Year.

1992 • September 24: Pedro makes his first major-league appearance.

O ⋆ L ⋆ O ⋆ G ⋆ Y

1993 • Pedro is traded to the Montreal Expos for Delino Deshields after his rookie season.

1997 • Pedro leads the National League in Complete Games and ERA; he wins the Cy Young Award.

1998 • Pedro signs the richest contract in baseball history after being traded to the Boston Red Sox.

1999 • Pedro wins the All-Star Game and is named All-Star MVP; he leads majors in Wins and ERA and wins the Cy Young Award again. He becomes just the third pitcher in history to win the Cy Young Award in both the American and National Leagues.

PEDRO MARTINEZ

Place of Birth **Manoguayabo, Dominican Republic**
Born **October 25, 1971**
Height **5′ 11″**
Weight **180 pounds**
College **Ohio Dominican College**
Minor League Player of the Year **1991**
N.L. Cy Young Award **1997**
A.L. Cy Young Award **1999**
All-Star Game MVP **1999**

★ MAJOR LEAGUE STATISTICS ★

Year	Team	Games	Innings	Wins–Losses	Strikeouts	ERA
1992	L.A. Dodgers	2	8	0–1	8	2.25
1993	L.A. Dodgers	65	107	10–5	119	2.61
1994	Montreal Expos	24	144 2/3	11–5	142	3.42
1995	Montreal Expos	30	194 2/3	14–10	174	3.51
1996	Montreal Expos	33	216 2/3	13–10	222	3.70
1997	Montreal Expos	31	241 1/3	17–8	305	1.90*
1998	Boston Red Sox	33	233 2/3	19–7	251	2.89
1999	Boston Red Sox	31	213 1/3	23*–4	313*	2.07*
2000	Boston Red Sox	29	217	18–6	284	1.74
2001	Boston Red Sox	18	116 2/3	7–3	163	2.39
2002	Boston Red Sox	30	199 1/3	20-4	239	2.26
2003	Boston Red Sox	29	186 2/3	14-4	206	2.22
Total		355	2,079	166-67	2,426	2.58

* Led Leagues

★ ★ ★

ABOUT THE AUTHOR

Mark Stewart has written hundreds of
features and more than fifty books about sports
for young readers. A nationally syndicated
columnist ("Mark My Words"), he lives and
works in New Jersey. For Children's Press,
Stewart is the author of more than twenty books
in the Sports Stars series, including biographies
of other baseball greats Mark McGwire, Bernie
Williams, and Ivan Rodriguez. He is also the
author of the Watts History of Sports, a six-
volume history of auto racing, baseball,
basketball, football, hockey, and soccer.